The New Novello Choral Edition

NOVELLO HANDEL EDITION

General Editor Watkins Shaw

Messiah

A Sacred Oratorio for soprano, alto, tenor and bass soli,
SATB and orchestra

Words compiled from Holy Scripture by Charles Jennens

Edited, and the orchestral accompaniment arranged for
performance with organ or for piano rehearsal, by Watkins Shaw

Vocal Score

NOVELLO

London and Sevenoaks

Cat. No. 07 0137

Publication of the revised edition of *Messiah* marks the end of Watkins Shaw's distinguished tenure (1972-91) as General Editor of the Novello Handel Edition. He is succeeded by Donald Burrows.

Also published by Novello in connection with this edition:

A Textual and Historical Companion to Handel's 'Messiah' by Watkins Shaw (Paperback 1982, ISBN 0 85360 033 3, Cat. No. 11 0122).
 '. . . a very solid, thoroughly scholarly book, full of information and sound judgment' (J.P. Larsen, *Handel's Messiah*, 2nd ed., 1972).

G. F. Handel, *MESSIAH*, ed. Watkins Shaw (Study score, Cat. No. 89 0031)

It is requested that on all concert notices and programmes acknowledgement is made to 'The New Novello Choral Edition (Shaw)'.

Orchestral material is available on hire or sale from the Publisher. Continuo part (2 copies required) available on hire.

NB The layout of bars and page numbers in The New Novello Choral Edition corresponds exactly to that in Novello's previous edition, for ease of reference in rehearsal when both may be in use.

CONTENTS

PREFACE

TO THE 1992 REVISED VOCAL SCORE

The vocal score of this edition first appeared in 1959, followed in 1965 by the full score, subsequently issued in reduced format as a 'study score'. Also in 1965 a related work, *A Textual and Historical Companion to Handel's 'Messiah'* by the present editor (hereafter *Textual Companion* for short) was published. This includes extensive discussion of the principal manuscripts (the autograph and so-called conducting score) together with details of numerous secondary manuscript sources and the earliest printed editions and a discussion of textual authority. In addition, by extensive treatment of the complex history of the work in the composer's lifetime, it explains the position of the alternative forms assumed by so many movements, and it also deals with Handel's methods of notation.

The opportunity afforded by the present welcome re-engraving (more strictly, 'new origination') of the vocal score has been taken to relieve its pages of certain features more relevant to a scholar's enquiries and an editor's conscience than to the general purposes of a vocal score, now that the study score, wherein these are scrupulously noted, is conveniently accessible.

Following my own clearance of a path through the jungle, contributions to *Messiah* studies in certain matters of important detail have been made by H. D. Clausen in *Haendels Direktionspartituren* (Hamburg, 1972) and in two perceptive articles by Donald Burrows, both in *Music & Letters*: 'Handel's performances of "Messiah": the evidence of the conducting score' (vol. 56 (1975), pp. 319-34) and 'The autographs and early copies of "Messiah": some further thoughts' (vol. 66 (1985), pp. 201-19). Insofar as these impinge on practical matters relevant to performances today (in particular the choice of variant movements) and slightly modify the *Textual Companion* in that regard, they are taken into account in the following notes, which treat of matters of immediate concern to the user of the edition, some of them more fully discussed in the *Textual Companion*. Fortunately, too, the 'Goldschmidt' MS (see *Textual Companion*, p. 79), whose contents I was formerly able to do no more than estimate, has now become accessible.

VARIANT VERSIONS: SELECTION AND USE

Including the division of 'He shall feed his flock/ Come unto him' between alto and soprano, but neglecting other, straightforward transpositions, no fewer than 11 movements (counting 'How beautiful are the feet/Their sound is gone out' as one for this reckoning) were subject to re-shaping or complete recomposition by Handel, some of them more than once, following original composition in 1741 and first performances in 1742. How is this quantity of material to be regarded today, and to what extent is it possible to judge how the composer would wish us to regard it?

While it is correct to say there is no single, final form of the work, that must not be taken glibly to mean that we may pick and choose as we please among all these variants. For it is perfectly evident that from 1750 there was a certain settling down, which, if not absolutely clear to us in every detail and still including some recognized alternatives as to voices used, justifies us in concluding that Handel had by then decidedly laid aside some of these variant forms. For purposes of this edition they have all been placed into one or other of three categories.

First are those for which there is every indication that they had been gradually abandoned by 1750. It does not seem to me proper to include them in a performing edition, however significant they may be for study or for use as illustrations to a historical discourse. If not an exact parallel, that would be akin, I suggest, to including in a performing edition of Mendelssohn's *Elijah* the original duet version of 'Lift thine eyes' or, of Elgar's Op.36, the version of the final variation used at the first performance. Attempts to re-enact the first performance of *Messiah*, or to resurrect the original structure (with da capo) of 'Rejoice greatly', or to use the da capo aria form of 'How beautiful are the feet/Their sound is gone out' and the *arioso* setting of 'But lo, the angel of the Lord', and so on, merely because they represent the work as it was in such-and-such a year, are to be deplored. They would, I believe, be a dis-service to the composer in a mistaken pursuit of novelty. I cannot agree even with so paramount an authority on Handel as Winton Dean when, after actually conceding that these are 'probably' rejected by Handel, he says '*Messiah* is performed so often that conductors might be encouraged to try everything' (*The Musical Times*, vol. 107 (1966), p. 157). Accordingly, certain alternative settings of Nos. 6, 14(b), 18, 36, 38/39, 43 and 50 are not included in this score. But it is entirely proper that they should be available for study, and they are therefore set out in the *Textual Companion*, while the modification of No. 3 is described on pp. 155-6 therein.

Next is a group of variants whose individual status is in varying degrees uncertain in the light of present knowledge. Taking a very broad view rather than rule them out entirely, they are included here, but in the form of an Appendix. However much one may deplore the use of words from Isaiah instead of Romans as intended by Jennens, the compiler of the libretto, there is just the most shadowy possibility that after its abandonment from 1745 Handel may have returned to the duet and chorus version of 'How beautiful are the feet' in a performance late in life, and perhaps also to the original bass setting of 'Thou art gone up on high'. (On a purely subjective, rather than historical view, as that and the later alto version are both so neutral in *affekt*, little of value is lost if the one is substituted for the other.) Uncertainty surrounds the exact date of composition of the alto setting in C minor of 'How beautiful are the feet' and the occasions on which it was performed. Written with Guadagni in mind, and therefore not earlier than 1750, it was nevertheless not used at Covent Garden performances in that year when he sang the newly-composed 'But who may abide the day of his coming?'. Dr Burrows suggests, however, that it may have been used at the Foundling Hospital performance of that year, about which we know little. In 1958 it seemed to me that it might well also have been sung by him at Covent Garden in 1753; but if so, then according to Burrows we are left with one more endorsement of Frasi's name on the soprano version in the conducting score than can be allotted to known occasions. Be all this as it may, this variant represents the latest of Handel's re-compositions in the work, and was certainly used by him, though whether later rejected or not we cannot say. One feels it may justifiably be used now and again to increase the alto role in Part Two, especially if No. 36 be omitted. Finally, there is the compound-time form of 'Rejoice greatly', whose inclusion here, it must be conceded, is inconsistent: for (*Textual Companion*, p. 125) I certainly believe that the common-time version – fashioned in 1745, not 1749 as previously estimated – was the composer's regular choice in the last ten years of his life. Strictly speaking, therefore, on my own classification the compound-time form should have been treated like the first category of variants listed in the paragraph immediately above. However, risking inconsistency, the 12/8 version seems so important a document in relation to the later common-time version that it may justifiably be made freely available to all users of the latter without the need to refer to the *Textual Companion*. It cannot be denied that there are moments in the common-time version at which one feels the original compound-time lilt remains integral to the thought.

This leaves the third category, what may be called the substantive alternatives found in the body of the edition. A few comments on each are called for.

1)   The sequence 'Then shall the eyes of the blind/ He shall feed his flock/Come unto him'. Having composed this in B flat for soprano (our Version I), Handel transposed it entire to F major for alto at the first performance at Dublin when it was sung by Mrs Cibber. He then hit upon the idea of dividing it between alto and soprano (our Version II), whereupon the all-alto version (not represented here, but available on hire from Novello) seems to have fallen into disuse, though Dr Burrows believes it was revived for one of the two Covent Garden performances of 1750. Version II was undoubtedly the more frequent in use, but in performances of

which we have precise information the all-soprano version was used at Covent Garden in 1752 and at the Foundling Hospital in 1754, so that it was clearly not abandoned by Handel.

2)   'But who may abide the day of his coming?' and 'Thou art gone up on high'. The idea of transposed versions of these (especially the former) for soprano may seem startling today in the light of long associations of a different sort, but it has Handel's unquestioned authority for his Foundling Hospital performance of 1754 and probably in 1755 too. It is to be noted, however, that he gave these, and also No. 52, to a special singer who did not undertake the remaining soprano solos. For the Foundling Hospital in 1754 he had 'But who may abide?' transposed to A minor, but the soprano-pitch version subsequently embodied in the late 'conducting score' (see *Textual Companion*, pp. 80, 159) put it in G minor as adopted here. The A Minor version (available on hire from Novello) involves some different octave adjustments from those in the string parts of that in G minor, and in bar 72 makes an interesting one in the voice part, suggested correspondingly here on p. 30 (cf. p.23).

3)   'If God be for us'. The transposition of this to C minor is also something still unaccustomed to those conditioned by the tradition of editions by Vincent Novello and Ebenezer Prout, yet it was particularly well established in Handel's alternative use. Though it lacks the ringing affirmation of soprano tone and pitch, it has the practical merit of giving the alto voice (whether man or woman) something important in Part Three.

4)   The 'Pastoral Symphony' and 'Why do the Nations?'. In programme notes and elsewhere I have more than once stressed that the shortened forms of these movements are not makeshifts devised by Handel merely to meet some emergency (see, for instance, my remark on p. 160 of earlier prints of this score). They have their own artistic validity no less than his authority in use. The short form of No. 40 almost certainly goes back to the first performances. Dr Burrows is inclined to consider that the short form of both may have been Handel's regular form from 1743 onwards, and I do not dissent though it cannot be absolutely proved. Had it not been for the publishers' entirely sensible wish to maintain the same page numbers as former prints of this score, I should have been inclined to move the longer forms to the Appendix. Nevertheless it has to be accepted that the longer form of No. 40, at least, is secure in popularity.

ALLOCATION OF VOICES, RECOMMENDATIONS FOR TODAY

By those transpositions of Nos. 6, 19/20, 36, and 52 Handel achieved a certain variety of timbre either within a performance or between one performance and another. He also did this in other ways and at various times. Thus, employing both a woman soprano and a boy treble, he not infrequently gave the latter Nos. 14-16 and 38. He also once made use of a boy for the entire normal soprano role. Again, he might treat what was originally the tenor sequence of Nos. 29-32 in any of the following ways:

	A	B	C	D
29:	Soprano	Soprano	Soprano	Tenor
30:	Soprano	Soprano	Soprano	Tenor
31:	Soprano	Tenor	Treble	Tr./Sop.
32:	Soprano	Tenor	Treble	Tr./Sop.

More elaborately, as we have seen, by means of transposition he devised roles for two sopranos on at least two occasions. One role, consisting of Nos. 18-20, 31-2, 38 (Version I), and 45, of a lyrical character, the other (Nos. 6, 36, and 52) more powerful and dramatic. Yet again he sometimes allotted all the alto-pitch movements (with or without the transposed form of No. 52) to a woman, sometimes to a man, and, in 1750, partly to one and partly to the other.

These explanations are the background to some practical recommendations for the present day.

It must first be emphasized that though Handel composed his alto-pitch settings of Nos. 6 and 36 with a male singer (Guadagni) in mind, he did not hesitate subsequently to allot them at that same pitch to a woman. Conversely, he sometimes gave the other alto-pitch movements which had originally been sung by a woman (including 'He was despised') to a man. The point is that the employment today of a countertenor, though sometimes extremely effective, is no touchstone of 'authenticity' in performance.

The employment of two sopranos (involving 'But who may abide?' at soprano pitch), though no doubt brilliantly effective and certainly known to have been adopted by Handel, is costly but could suitably mark some distinctive occasion.

Similarly the simultaneous employment of both a man and a woman alto is expensive. If, for some special performance it is possible to adopt it, then Nos. 6 and 36 at least must go to the man, taking the occasion perhaps to give him Version II (Appendix) of No. 38 also.

No one need be in the least apologetic for using only the simple 'standard' quartet of soloists, whether the alto be man or woman, taking either form of No. 52 according to taste while not forgetting the good claims of Version II.

One might well adopt one or other of the possible varied allocations of Nos. 29-32 as shown above; and if a good boy singer is available there is a strong artistic case for allotting him the nativity scene, Nos. 14-16, set apart from the rest of the work as its only piece of scriptural narrative.

PERFORMANCE OF RECITATIVE

1)   The *appoggiature* here given are the editorial representation of the unwritten conventions. If within round brackets, they take the place of the succeeding main note.

2)   *Recitativo secco* should be delivered at the pace and in the natural manner of speech. The written note- and rest-values (especially the latter) are only intended to make the contents of the bar look grammatical. In *Messiah* particularly (and this applies strongly to No. 8) a tendency towards sanctimony has grown up, assisted by sustained harmonies and counting the beats. In the accompaniments here intended for organ (where the true continuo part on hire for use with orchestra is of course for harpsichord) an attempt has been made to let a little air into the texture to encourage a lighter delivery.

3)   In 1959 the long-standing convention was unchallenged whereby, despite the strict notation of the bar, the cadence chords at the ends of recitatives were held up until after the soloist had finished, and they were so treated when this edition appeared in that year. Subsequently this convention was challenged by J. A. Westrup who, by a firmly based historical argument, reasoned that this was not always so, even though a harmonic clash might result ('The cadence in baroque recitative', *Natalicia Musicologica Knud Jeppeson oblata*, Copenhagen, 1962).

But the matter is not so conclusive as some people rather excitedly and dogmatically began to suppose. Handel's contemporary Telemann (*Singe-und Generalbass Uebungen*, 1733-5) drew a distinction between cadences in opera (non-postponed) and cantata (postponed: 'in cantaten aber pfleget man sie nachzuschlagen'). This brings up the awkward question of which category *Messiah*, with obvious operatic roots, belongs to. The subject receives balanced consideration by Robert Donington in *A Performer's Guide to Baroque Music* (1973) and *The Interpretation of Music* (New Version, 1974). He regards the tradition of postponement as 'standard convention', the other as 'an undoubted option', the 'interesting case for which should not be pressed too far'. I agree with him that the deciding factor is one of pace of transition from one movement to another (clearly important in opera), and this, in the last resort, is a matter of taste.

In the present score Handel's written notation of this feature is undisturbed, leaving its treatment to individual judgement, though in the full score (1965) and parts the older tradition remains accounted for. Where thought fit, this should be adjusted in performance. Performers are free to decide for themselves; but if I were asked, then (as a matter of taste, not historical knowledge) I would probably suggest the non-postponed form in No. 2, and certainly recommend it without hesitation in No. 15 where the forward movement to No. 16 is surely paramount. But, if nowhere else, I should prefer the postponed form in No. 8 in order to leave the impressive words uncovered.

CON/SENZA RIPIENO DIRECTIONS

The conducting score contains *con ripieno* and *senza ripieno* directions in the instrumental parts in the composer's hand. My surmise in the *Textual Companion* (p. 41) that they were added in 1749 has proved correct. But not only do they give the impression of markedly decreasing attention to detail as the work proceeds, but they are curious in some other respects (ibid., pp. 56-7); moreover, they did not pass into two important MSS copied from this score after 1749. It has now been shown by H. D. Clausen that their validity extended only to the conditions of Handel's performance in that one year. They are not reproduced in this vocal score, but will be found for information and study in the full score, and also, should any conductor wish to use them, in the orchestral parts to this edition.

ORNAMENTATION

Handel's own (very few) explicit shake-marks (**tr**) are straightforwardly reproduced. Mid-eighteenth-century ornamentation as given in the 'Goldschmidt' and 'Matthews' MSS (for which see *Textual Companion*) will be found, clearly shown as such, in Nos. 3, 18 (Version I), 23, 32, 45, and 52 (Version I). A 'grace' from 'Matthews' to No. 18 (Version II), which could not be conveniently expressed otherwise is given below, together with an alternative to the 'Goldschmidt' gracing of the cadence of No. 3. This is a pencil addition of unknown date, not by Handel, in the conducting score. All other *appoggiature*, 'graces', and shakes are editorial suggestions only (the last in square brackets). In recitative the introduction of *appoggiature* is a recognized traditional feature of style. Otherwise, ornamentation being a spontaneous matter, these suggestions must not be regarded as hard and fast, and should be changed and freely supplemented at discretion.

No. 3. Cadenza at bar 73 from Bodleian MS Tenbury 346. See p.10.

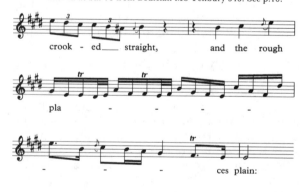

No. 18 (Version II). Cadenza at bar 99 from 'Matthews' MS. See p.237.

RHYTHMIC INTERPRETATION

The editor has made his suggestions for the interpretation of the loose rhythmic notation of the eighteenth century in these ways:
1) Wherever the following notation is found ♩.. ♪ or ⅞. ♪ it is to be understood that the original sources read ♩. ♪ or ⅞ ♪. Neither double dots nor dotted rests were used by Handel, his scribes, or publishers. On the other hand, the notation ⅞ ⅞ ♪ is Handel's.

2) Other alterations are suggested by rhythmic signs placed above or below Handel's notation. These signs consist of the usual notation without the note-head itself, thus: | |. ♪ ♫ ⌐ ⌐ In all instances, whether of (1) or (2) therefore, Handel's notation either is preserved exactly or can be readily reconstructed.
3) Horizontal square brackets are editorial marks of regrouping in triple time.

EDITORIAL FORMALITIES

Numbering of movements is editorial. Original C clefs for chorus soprano, alto, and tenor parts are transcribed in the G clef, while original clefs of solo movements are shown on a preliminary stave. The present time signature 4/4 invariably represents Handel's **C** which is retained as the purely conventional signature for *recitativo secco*. Barring and 'underlaying' of words are fully discussed in the *Textual Companion*. In the voice parts, words in *italic* represent editorial suggestions or emendations. With regard to transposed forms of movements authorized by Handel, he did not write out the transpositions himself. They were the work of his scribes, in the course of which small differences of verbal underlay occurred. In my opinion these have no integral authority as alternatives, and I have uniformly applied the underlay of the composer's original forms. I bow to the current general wish to eliminate the vocal slurs of 1959, showing syllabification, even though I consider they might be helpful to the reader, as for example at bar 42, page 43.

Handel's dynamic marks, however he expressed them, are standardized in modern form, while editorial supplementation is within square brackets (a different method is adopted in the full score). Any other material in square brackets is editorial. Unlike the earlier issues of this vocal score, Handel's unsystematic instrumental slurs and staccato wedges are now extended to precisely comparable phrases within any movement without editorial differentiation, and any missing accidentals (which are never in doubt) are supplied likewise. Both these forms of editorial activity are made plain in the study score which also furnishes Handel's sparse figuring of the basso continuo not shown here.

THE KEYBOARD PART

In any vocal score the keyboard reduction of the orchestral score obviously must serve the purpose of pianoforte rehearsals. But, conscious as I was in 1959 that *Messiah*, more than any other such work, received frequent performances accompanied by organ alone in lieu of orchestra, I attempted what I described as the 'admittedly thankless' task of devising an arrangement which, while still being useful for pianoforte rehearsal, yet gave somewhat more assistance to organists than earlier editors of vocal scores had provided.

The then music critic of *The Times* (26 June 1959) deplored this intention. Bearing this magisterial stricture in mind when preparing the present revised vocal score, and also feeling doubtful whether 'organ only' performances were still sufficiently frequent to make such a dual task worth attempting, I raised the question in 1990 in the columns of *Church Music Quarterly* and *The Organists' Review*. A copious response left no shadow of doubt that such performances are still very plentiful and worth catering for, and, what is more, that my keyboard part had been found helpful in this regard (without, apparently, upsetting pianists as *The Times* prophesied).

Now, therefore, I have retained this feature while trying to carry its principles a little further, more frequently choosing idioms suited to the organ but playable on the piano, rather than pianoforte idioms (particularly tremolando and arpeggiation assisted by sustaining pedal, or rhythmically reiterated triads) unsuited to the organ.

PIANO REHEARSAL: Where, dealing in terms of left hand and organ pedals, there is more on the lower stave than a pianist's left hand can grasp, and the right hand is not free to lend assistance, the arrangement is such that it will be found perfectly adequate for rehearsal purposes if the left hand neglects the notes with upward stems and plays the bass line only, though in No. 20 ('He shall feed his flock') it will often be convenient to take the bass an octave higher on the piano in order to play the complete texture.

'ORGAN ONLY' PERFORMANCE: Handel's orchestra used double basses with cellos throughout, except for one phrase in 'Comfort ye'. Nevertheless, I have suggested some passages to be played without pedals as a relief from organ 16 ft. tone. In the four choruses which Handel worked up from duets composed earlier, and which retain a good deal of duet texture, my suggestions for manuals only are intended to reflect this lightness of texture, and to heighten the effect of fuller choral passages by re-entry of the organ pedals. All these mere suggestions can, of course, be ignored, just as, contrariwise, some pedal passages (e.g., in No. 2) might be played simply coupled to manual at 8 ft. pitch only. This is perhaps particularly true of arias whose instrumentation is for unison violins and basso continuo, as No. 45.

Small-size notation has been used to suggest the continuo filling-in of the texture, but one is hampered by not having a third stave on which to express it more adequately or in a more suitable part of the register. One hopes organists will adjust this for themselves in performance on the basis of what is actually given. (For performances with orchestra a completely independent continuo part is on hire.) With regard to what is instrumental obbligato, in full-size notes, it is necessary to explain that I have not treated the oboe parts (which, except in No. 39, the composer did not supply himself) as such, so that when oboes alone play in unison with the voices they are not reproduced in full size as part of the keyboard arrangement: see, for instance, bars 1 – 5 of No. 21, 'His yoke is easy', where oboes double chorus sopranos.

With regard to many arias, the use of pedals (whether 16 or 8 ft.) frees the left hand to supply, on a second manual, this impression of continuo harmony while the right hand brings out an obbligato violin part shown in full-size notes. But alternatively it is sometimes perfectly possible to achieve a satisfactory effect by playing the bass part and the violin part on manuals only as two-part texture without harmonic filling-in, as, e.g., Nos. 18, 32, 43, or 45.

The treatment of the two 'rage' arias, Nos. 6 and 40, will be noted – chords for organ rather than tremolando for pianoforte. Some performers may prefer an adaptation of their own after consulting the study score. Elsewhere I have not hesitated at certain points to simplify the texture where the effect of brilliance and movement can be adequately conveyed without the complication of chains of thirds and (especially) sixths. To avoid a certain hardness of articulation when *allegro* semiquavers double voices (quite different on the organ from the silkier effect of strings) I have sometimes slightly modified the outline. And at certain climactic *forte* passages where the strings are in a register well above the chorus voices, I have brought these down an octave on the assumption that 4 ft. stops at least will have been drawn. Salient instances occur in Nos. 33 and 35. There may be other points (say bars 53-6 of No. 3) at which organists might wish to use discretion (according to registration) to avoid shrillness.

ACKNOWLEDGEMENTS

When originally working on this edition I was indebted to H.M. Queen Elizabeth II for gracious permission to use Handel's original MS score, and to St Michael's College, Tenbury, Worcs., for the use of his MS conducting score. These documents on which the edition is based are now respectively the property of the British Library (RM 20.f.2) and the Bodleian Library, Oxford (MSS Tenbury 346-7). I am also grateful to the Pierpont Morgan Library, New York and Archbishop Marsh's Library, Dublin for permission to use ornamentation from Cary MS 122 ('Goldschmidt' MS) and MS Z1.2.26 ('Matthews' MS) respectively.

In now bringing to its close all the work I have been privileged to do on Handel's music over the past 36 years I cannot fail to express my gratitude for the consideration continuously extended by the firm of Novello and Co., beginning when it was still a family firm under Harold Brooke, and for its allowing me a liberal interpretation of an editor's duties; the helpfulness of its successive officers, engravers, copy-editors, and proof-readers; the many valued friendships the work has brought me; and the generous reception of my endeavours.

WATKINS SHAW, Worcester, June 1991

ADDITIONAL NOTE

A very useful facsimile of the conducting score (Bodleian Library, MSS Tenbury 346-7) was published in 1974 by the Scolar Press. Those who wish to study this for themselves should note that, as detailed in the *Textual Companion*, the non-autograph portions contain certain scribal errors, and that at various dates in Handel's lifetime it must have contained, as loose inserts, alternative settings and transpositions not included in it by the time of his death, some of which are now bound with RM 20.f.2 in the British Library and others are now lost.

Furthermore, the facsimile fails to show the following singers' names: 'Stor*er*' ('Ev'ry valley', MS 346, f. 4*v*); '*Mrs* Clive' ('And suddenly there was with the angel', MS 346, f. 60*v*); 'Francesina' ('Behold, and see', MS 347, f. 39*v*); while 'Sigra Avolio' on 'Thy rebuke' (MS 347, f. 38*v*) is blurred and 'Sigra Frasi' written over 'the Boy' in 'He was cut off' (MS 347, f. 40*v*) fails to show in red.

MAJORA CANAMUS

(Virgil, *Eclogue IV*)

And without Controversy, great is the mystery of Godliness:

> *God was manifested in the Flesh, justified by the Spirit, seen of Angels, preached among the Gentiles, believed on in the world, received up in glory.*

In whom are hid all the Treasures of Wisdom and Knowledge.

(1 Timothy iii, 16; Colossians ii, 3)

These words, selected by Jennens, the librettist, formed a preface to the word-book of the first performance in April 1742, at Dublin. They were repeated on the word-books published in London 1749-59 and later.

PART ONE

SINFONY [*OVERTURE*]

2

No. 2   Recitative   **COMFORT YE**

Isaiah xl, 1–3

C

The voice of him that crieth in the wil-der-ness, Pre-pare ye the way of the

Lord, make straight in the des-ert a high-way for our God.

30

34

[attacca]

No. 3 Air EV'RY VALLEY SHALL BE EXALTED

Isaiah xl, 4

Andante

TENOR

A

Ev - 'ry val - ley, ev - 'ry val - ley

5

9

---

* For recitative cadences, see p.vii.

† For an extra bar originally found between present bars 5 and 6 (also 7/8, 80/81, 82/83) which Handel wisely eliminated after 1742,
see *Textual Companion*, p.155.

7

* For cadenza, see p.viii.

No. 4   Chorus   AND THE GLORY OF THE LORD

Isaiah xl, 5

12

14

No. 5   Recitative   THUS SAITH THE LORD

Haggai ii, 6–7; Malachi iii, 1

earth, the sea, the dry land, all na-tions, I'll shake, and the de-

16

-sire of all

19

B

na - tions shall come: the Lord, whom ye seek, shall sud-den-ly come to his

22

tem-ple, ev'n the mes-sen-ger of the co - ve-nant, whom ye de - light in:

25

be-hold, he shall come, saith the Lord of hosts.

28

[attacca]

No. 6   Air   BUT WHO MAY ABIDE THE DAY OF HIS COMING?

Malachi iii, 2   *VERSION I * (The third Version to be composed)*

*Composed in 1750 for the male alto (counter–tenor), Gaetano Guadagni. The version originally composed for bass in 1741, substantially different, was thereafter disused by Handel and is not represented here.

22

*Handel himself wrote both notes.

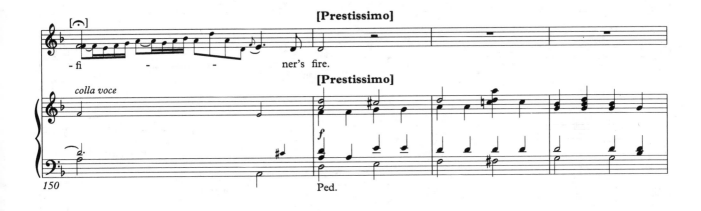

(to p.35)

No. 6   *VERSION II (Transposition of Version I for Soprano)**

*Material in A minor (score, vocal score and parts) is available on hire from Novello for exceptional use if required. See p.vi.

un poco piano

32

34

No. 7   Chorus   AND HE SHALL PURIFY

Malachi iii, 3

36

*Alto: autograph reads

No. 8   Recitative   BEHOLD, A VIRGIN SHALL CONCEIVE

Isaiah vii, 14; Matthew i, 23

No. 9   Air and Chorus   O THOU THAT TELLEST GOOD TIDINGS TO ZION

Isaiah xl, 9; lx, 1

C

O thou that tell-est good ti - dings to Je-ru - sa - lem, lift

up thy voice with strength; lift it up, be not a -

D

- fraid; say un - to the cit - ies of Ju - dah, say un - to the

cit - ies of Ju - dah, Be - hold___ your God!___ be - hold___ your God! say

44

* There is a sign here which may be '*p*' or '*tr*'.

[*] This doubling is perhaps better omitted in performances with organ accompaniment alone.

glo - ry of the Lord_____ is ris - en up - on thee.

Lord_____ is ris - en up - on thee.

glo - ry of the Lord_____ is ris - en up - on thee.

glo - ry of the Lord_____ is ris - en up - on thee.

135

8ft.
ad lib.

L

139

143

147

No. 10   Recitative   FOR, BEHOLD, DARKNESS SHALL COVER THE EARTH

Isaiah lx, 2–3

- ry shall be seen up - on thee, and his glo - ry shall be seen up - on thee.

And the Gen-tiles shall come to thy light, and kings to the bright-ness of thy ris - ing.

No. 11   Air   THE PEOPLE THAT WALKED IN DARKNESS

Isaiah ix, 2

Larghetto

The peo - ple that walk - ed in dark - ness, that walk - ed in dark -

- ness, the peo - ple that walk - ed, that walk - ed in dark-ness have

* Handel wrote both notes.

52

D

up - on___ them__ hath the__ light__ shin - ed,

Ped.

and they__ that__ dwell,___ that dwell__ in the land__ of the

p

Man.

sha - - dow of death, up - on___ them hath the

light_____ shin - - ed, up - on___ them hath the light__ shin - ed.

f

Ped. Man. Ped. Man.

Ped.

No. 12   Chorus   FOR UNTO US A CHILD IS BORN

Isaiah ix, 6

56

58

No. 13 PIFA [*PASTORAL SYMPHONY*]

VERSION I – Bars 1–11 only
VERSION II – Complete (in this Version
omit bar 11 until the *Da Capo*)

No. 14a   Recitative   THERE WERE SHEPHERDS ABIDING IN THE FIELD

Luke ii, 8

No. 14b   Recitative   AND, LO, THE ANGEL OF THE LORD CAME UPON THEM

Luke ii, 9

No. 15   Recitative   AND THE ANGEL SAID UNTO THEM

Luke ii, 10–11

No. 16   Recitative   AND SUDDENLY THERE WAS WITH THE ANGEL

Luke ii, 13

No. 17   Chorus   GLORY TO GOD

Luke ii, 14

No. 18   Air   REJOICE GREATLY, O DAUGHTER OF ZION

Zechariah ix, 9–10   *VERSION I (The third Version to be composed)**

*Vocal ornaments not in square brackets from 'Matthews' MS. See appendix for $\frac{12}{8}$ version.

*Grace notes from the Autograph.

No. 19 Recitative **THEN SHALL THE EYES OF THE BLIND***

Isaiah xxxv, 5–6 *VERSION I*

VERSION II

* Material for a third version of Nos. 19 and 20 (score, vocal score and parts) for Alto *throughout* is available on hire from Novello for exceptional use if required. See p.vi.

80

Air HE SHALL FEED HIS FLOCK LIKE A SHEPHERD

Isaiah xl, 11; Matthew xi, 28–29 *VERSION I*

* See p.ix on the subject of the keyboard part.

No. 20   *VERSION II*

* See p.ix on the subject of the keyboard part.

VERSION I

VERSION II

No. 21   Chorus   HIS YOKE IS EASY

Matthew xi, 30

B

yoke___ is__ ea - - - sy, his bur - then is light,

his yoke___ is___

- sy, his bur-then is light,___ his bur - then, his bur - then is light,

his bur - then is light,___ his

B

his

ea - - - - sy, his bur-then is

yoke___ is__ ea - - - - sy,

bur-then is light,___ his bur-then, his bur-then, his bur - then is

light,___ his bur-then, his bur - then is light, his bur - then is

his bur-then is light,___ his

his bur-then, his bur-then, his bur - then, his

90

PART TWO

No. 22

Chorus   BEHOLD THE LAMB OF GOD

John i, 29

94

Air   HE WAS DESPISED *

Isaiah liii, 3; 1,6

*Vocal ornaments from 'Goldschmidt' MS except in bars 42 and 67 which are editorial.

sor-rows, and ac - quaint - ed with grief:

[colla voce]

Man.

Ped.

FINE

E

He gave his back to the smi - ters,

un poco piano

he gave his back to the smi - ters, and his cheeks to

them that pluck - ed off the hair, and his cheeks to

No. 24   Chorus   SURELY HE HATH BORNE OUR GRIEFS

Isaiah liii, 4–5

* Handel's key-signature had three flats only; he used accidentals for D flats.

-tise - ment of____ our peace____

the chas - tise - ment of our peace

-tise - - ment of our peace____

the chas - tise - ment of our peace

was up - on him;

was____ up - on____ him;

____ was____ up - on____ him;

was____ up - on him;

21

23

25

[tr]

[attacca]

No. 25 Chorus   AND WITH HIS STRIPES WE ARE HEALED

Isaiah liii, 5

*Handel's key-signature had three flats only. His time-signature was ¢ with bars of varying length.

* Handel himself wrote both notes.
† Note slight change from earlier forms of this edition in the italicized editorially suggested words.

[attacca]

No. 26   Chorus   ALL WE LIKE SHEEP HAVE GONE ASTRAY

Isaiah liii, 6

112

* Alto: Handel himself wrote both notes.

No. 27   Recitative   ALL THEY THAT SEE HIM LAUGH HIM TO SCORN

Psalm xxii, 7 (*Book of Common Prayer*)

No. 28   Chorus   HE TRUSTED IN GOD

Psalm xxii, 8 (*Book of Common Prayer and A.V.*)

* Bracketed words from the Autograph.

Man. only *ad lib.*

No. 29   Recitative   THY REBUKE HATH BROKEN HIS HEART

Psalm lxix, 21 (*Book of Common Prayer*)

[attacca]

No. 30   Air   BEHOLD, AND SEE IF THERE BE ANY SORROW

Lamentations i, 12

* Handel's *appoggiatura*

124

No. 31   Recitative HE WAS CUT OFF OUT OF THE LAND OF THE LIVING

Isaiah liii, 8

He was cut off out of the land of the liv - ing: for the trans - gres - sion of thy peo - ple was he strick - en.

[attacca]

No. 32   Air BUT THOU DIDST NOT LEAVE HIS SOUL IN HELL *

Psalm xvi, 10

But thou didst not leave his soul in_____ hell, but thou didst not leave his

* Vocal ornaments from 'Matthews' MS.

No. 33   Chorus   LIFT UP YOUR HEADS, O YE GATES *

Psalm xxiv, 7–10

---

* In this chorus the division of the alto part is editorial: the style clearly requires the antiphony of *cori spezzati* in the Venetian manner. The division into semi–chorus and chorus, also editorial, is based on the word-books issued in connection with Handel's Covent Garden performances. (Handel himself adapted this chorus to form an orchestral *Concerto a due cori*.)

128

* The 1st Alto part should include any male singers available.

131

132

No. 34   Recitative   UNTO WHICH OF THE ANGELS SAID HE AT ANY TIME

Hebrews i, 5

No. 35   Chorus   LET ALL THE ANGELS OF GOD WORSHIP HIM

Hebrews i, 6

* Tenor: Handel himself wrote both notes.

136

* Tenor: Handel himself wrote both notes.

No. 36

Air   THOU ART GONE UP ON HIGH

VERSION I (*The third Version to be composed*)

* See *Textual Companion*

a - mong them, that the Lord God_____ might____

dwell_____ a - mong them,

that the Lord, the Lord God might____ dwell_____ a - mong them.

(to p.146)

VERSION II (Transposition of Version I for Soprano) *

144

Thou art gone up on high, thou art gone up on high, thou hast led cap-ti - vi-ty cap-tive, thou hast led cap-ti - vi-ty cap-tive, and re- cei - - ved, and re-cei-ved gifts for men: and re-cei-ved gifts for thine en-e-mies, that the Lord God might dwell a-mong them, and might dwell

No. 37   Chorus   THE LORD GAVE THE WORD

Psalm lxviii, 11 (*Book of Common Prayer*)

149

No. 38   Aria   HOW BEAUTIFUL ARE THE FEET *

Romans x, 15   VERSION I

* See Appendix and *Textual Companion*, pp. 112–13, 117.

preach the gos-pel of peace, and bring glad ti - dings, and

12

bring glad ti - - dings, glad ti - dings of good things, and

14

B

bring glad ti - dings, glad ti - dings of good things, and bring_____ glad ti - dings, glad

16

ti - dings of ___ good things, glad ti - dings of ___ good things!

Man.   Ped.

19

[attacca]

22

No. 39   Chorus   THEIR SOUND IS GONE OUT

Romans x, 18   *VERSION I (The third Version to be composed)*

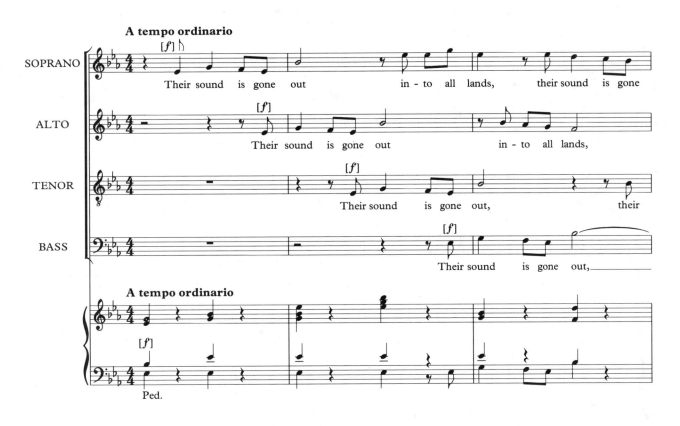

No. 40　　　Air　WHY DO THE NATIONS SO FURIOUSLY RAGE TOGETHER?

Psalm ii, 1–2 (*Book of Common Prayer*)　　　*VERSIONS I and II*

Why　　　do the na - tions　so　fu - rious - ly rage— to -

-ge - ther: why do the peo - ple i - ma - gine a vain

thing? Why do the na - tions rage___

so

[Man. *ad lib.*]

fu - rious - ly___ to - ge - ther: why

Ped.

do the peo-ple i - ma___

B

-gine a vain thing? i - ma - - -

-gine a vain thing?

Why do the na - tions so fu - rious-ly rage___ to -

- ge - ther: and why do the peo - ple, and

why do the peo - ple i - ma - gine a___ vain___

* For Version II (see p.vi) continue at the Recitative on p.160. Note–heads without stems indicate succeeding chord to facilitate page–turning.

158

thing? Why do the na - tions rage _____

48

51

C

so fu-rious-ly to - ge-ther, so fu-rious-ly to - ge - ther: and

54

Man. only *ad lib.*

Ped.

why do the peo-ple i - ma - gine a vain

57

thing? i - ma - - - gine a vain

60

160

VERSION II *

* This is not to be thought of as a makeshift ending, but an alternative with authority from Handel's own time. It leads dramatically to the following chorus.

No. 41   Chorus   LET US BREAK THEIR BONDS ASUNDER

Psalm ii, 3

let us break their bonds a - sun - der, let___ us, let___ us break,

- sun - der, let us break their

let us break their bonds a - sun - der, let___ us break, let us break their

- sun - der, let us break their bonds a -

29

C

let us break their bonds a - sun - der, their bonds a - sun - der, and cast

bonds, let us break their bonds,___ their bonds a - sun - der,

bonds, let us break their bonds a - sun - der, and cast a -

- sun - der, let us break their bonds a - sun - der,

C

Man.

32

a - way___ their yokes from

- way,___ and cast a - way,___

and cast a - way___

Ped.

36

No. 42   Recitative   HE THAT DWELLETH IN HEAVEN

Psalm ii, 4 (*Book of Common Prayer*)

He that dwell-eth in hea-ven shall laugh them to scorn: the Lord shall have them in de-ri-sion.

No. 43   Air   THOU SHALT BREAK THEM

Psalm ii, 9

Thou shalt break them, thou shalt break them with a rod of i-ron;

* Bar 38. See *Textual Companion*, p.179.

No. 44   Chorus HALLELUJAH

Rev. xix, 6; xi, 15; xix, 16

172

176

178

* Alto: Handel himself wrote both notes.

PART THREE

No. 45　　　　　　Air　I KNOW THAT MY REDEEMER LIVETH *

Job xix, 25–26; Cor. xv, 20

* The ornament in bar 42 is Handel's. Other vocal ornaments from 'Goldschmidt' MS, supplemented by 'Matthews' (*a*) and the editor (*b*).

184

* This is Handel's original form,
which he afterwards changed to

first - fruits of them that sleep,

etc.

* This is Handel's original form, which he afterwards changed to

first - fruits of them that sleep.

† Handel's text is as follows, with nothing to show how 'them' and 'that' are to be treated.

the first-fruits of them that sleep.

J.C. Smith, in the first fair copy (O) hazarded

the first - fruits of them that sleep.

The present Editor ventures a reading of his own, close to that in Add. MS 5062.

No. 46   Chorus   SINCE BY MAN CAME DEATH

I Cor. xv, 21–22

No. 47   Recitative   BEHOLD, I TELL YOU A MYSTERY

I Cor. xv, 51–52

No. 48   Air   THE TRUMPET SHALL SOUND

I Cor. xv, 52–54

* Ignoring small size notes.

190

* Handel wrote
rais'd— in - cor - rup - ti-ble

* Handel wrote: (see also bars 91–93)

in - cor - rup - ti-ble

† Handel wrote: (see also bars 94–96)

in - cor - rup - ti-ble

192

The trum-pet_ shall_ sound,___ the trum-pet_ shall_ sound,_____ and the dead shall_ be_ raised,_____ be raised_ in - cor - rup-ti-ble, be raised in - cor - rup-ti-ble, and we shall be changed, be changed,_____ and

Man. only *ad lib.* *

* Ignoring small size notes.

194

No. 49   Recitative   THEN SHALL BE BROUGHT TO PASS

I Cor. xv, 54

Nos. 50–51   Duet   O DEATH, WHERE IS THY STING?

I Cor. xv, 55–57   Chorus   BUT THANKS BE TO GOD

* For a discussion of bar 12, see *Textual Companion*, p.183.

vic - to-ry? The sting___ of__ death is sin;___ the sting of death is sin; and___

vic - to-ry? The sting___ of__ death is sin;___ and the__

16

___ the strength of sin is___ the law, the sting___

strength of sin___ is___ the law, the sting___ of__ death is sin,___ the

19

___ of__ death is sin;___ and the__ strength of sin___ is___ the law,

sting of death is sin;___ and___ the strength of sin is___ the law,

22

Ped.
Segue Chorus

No. 51 Chorus

No. 52   Air   IF GOD BE FOR US

Romans viii, 31, 33–34   *VERSION I* *

* Vocal ornaments not in square brackets from 'Goldschmidt' MS.

† Handel wrote   God be for us   ** Handel wrote   God is for us

206

right hand of God, who is at the right hand of God, at the right hand of

Adagio * [a tempo]

God, who makes in - ter - ces - sion for us.

Man. Ped.

(to p.217)

* Handel wrote

- ces - sion for

No. 52 *VERSION II (Transposition of Version I for Alto)* *

* Vocal ornaments applied from Version I.

for us, who can be a - gainst us?

B

Who shall lay___ a - ny - thing to the charge of

God's_ e - lect?_____ of God's_ e - lect?

who shall lay a - ny - thing to the charge_____

of_ God's e - lect?

214

right hand of God, who is at the right hand of God, at the right hand of

152

Adagio   **[a tempo]**

God,   who makes in - ter - ces - sion for   us.

Adagio   **[a tempo]**

Man.   Ped.

158

164

169

174

No. 53   Chorus   WORTHY IS THE LAMB THAT WAS SLAIN

Rev. v, 12–13

* Bar 39. It has been shown by Donald Burrows that this 'cut' relates to Handel's performance of 1743.

224

[attacca]

228

APPENDIX

Air   REJOICE GREATLY, O DAUGHTER OF ZION

Zechariah ix, 9–10

VERSION II (The second Version to be composed)

* Handel's own common–time notation of this $\frac{12}{8}$ bass has been preserved here. Crotchets, crotchet rests and minims should be read as dotted:

* Sing 'com'th'.
† Here Handel cut out 48 bars of the original form of this movement, and slightly changed the following bar to the form now given.

* In its original form this bar simply contained the harmony of D minor for voice and continuo only, followed by the direction 'Da Capo'. Handel altered it as now given to provide a link to a modified re-statement (bars 66 to first half of 69) of the opening (cf. bars 1–3 and 9–11), and then proceeded to use the last 39 bars of the section cut out as marked at bar 44 above.

236

shout, O daugh-ter of Je - ru - sa-lem: be-hold, thy__

King com - eth un - to thee, re - joice,__

re - joice,__ and shout,__

shout,__ shout,__ shout,__ re - joice__

great - ly, re - joice__

great - ly, O daugh - ter of Zi - on; shout, _____ O daugh - ter of Je -

- ru - sa - lem: be - hold, thy King cometh un - to thee, be - hold, thy
[sic]

Man.

Adagio [tr] [a tempo]

King com - eth un - to thee.

Adagio [a tempo]

Ped.

(to p.79)

* For cadenzas, see p.viii.

[No. 36]

Air   THOU ART GONE UP ON HIGH

Psalm lxviii, 18
(*Book of Common Prayer*)

VERSION III (*The first Version to be composed*)

C

might dwell a - mong them.

Thou art gone up on high, thou art gone up on high, thou hast

led cap - ti - vi - ty cap - tive, thou hast led cap - ti - vi - ty cap - tive,

and re - ceiv - ed gifts for men: yea, ev - en

for thine en - - - - -

God might dwell a - mong_ them, might dwell_____

98

a - mong____

103

F

them, that the Lord God might dwell a - mong them.

109 Man. Ped.

115

[tr]

120 (to p.146)

[No. 38]
Romans x, 15

Air HOW BEAUTIFUL ARE THE FEET
VERSION II

* These *appoggiature* are from the source. Handel's autograph copy of this version does not survive. See *Textual Companion*, p.186.

beau - ti - ful are the feet, how beau - ti - ful are the feet__ of them that

preach_ the gos - pel of peace, how beau - ti - ful are the feet__ of them that

preach_ the gos - pel of peace, how beau - ti - ful, how

beau - ti - ful are the feet___ of them that preach_ the gos - pel of peace, and

B

bring glad ti - dings, and bring glad ti - dings, glad

(to p.151)

246

[cf. No. 38] Duet and Chorus   HOW BEAUTIFUL ARE THE FEET

Isaiah lii, 7, 9 *

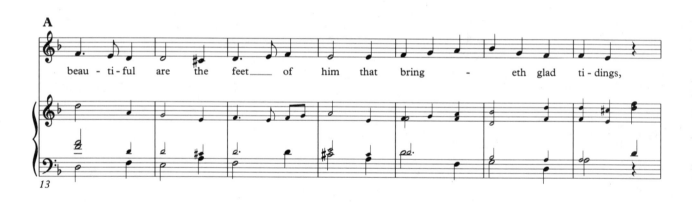

* Except inconsistently (at bars 110 and 112) Handel chose 'glad' where Isaiah reads 'good'.

†When desired, this part may be sung by a soprano, observing the octave transpositions noted. In such case the octave transpositions noted in bars 40–43 of Alto 1 must also be observed. This has Handel's authority.

248

250

D

him that bring - eth *glad* ti - dings, that bring - eth
(good)

How beau - ti - ful are the feet___ of him that bring - eth

how beau - ti - ful are the feet that

bring - eth *glad* ti - dings, that bring - eth
(good)

D

110

ti - dings of___ sal - va - - tion;

ti - dings of sal - va - tion, of___ sal - va - tion;

bring ti - dings of sal - va - tion, of sal - va - tion;

ti - dings of___ sal - va - - tion;

116

that saith___ un - to

that saith un - to

that saith___ un - to

that saith___ un - to

122

(to p.151 or 155)

[No. 39]   Air   THEIR SOUND IS GONE OUT

Romans x, 18   *VERSION II (The second Version to be composed)*

Their sound is gone out,_____ their sound is gone

out   in - to all__ lands,   in - to all__ lands,

and their words   un - to the ends   of the world,   and their

words un-to the ends of the world,

their sound is gone out in-to all lands, and their

words un-to the ends of the world, and their

words un-to the ends of the world.

(to p.155)

Published by Novello & Company Limited
Printed in the U.S.A.